Champagne Musher,

Rosemary Finley

CHAMPAGNE... Uncorked!

THE INSIDER'S GUIDE TO CHAMPAGNE!

ROSEMARY ZRALY

Champagne. . . Uncorked!

Edited, Designed, and Manufactured by

Favorite Recipes® Press

P.O. Box 305142

Nashville, Tennessee 37230

1-800-358-0560

Published by

RMZ Publications

157 East 57th St.

New York, New York 10022

1-800-830-9588

Library of Congress Catalogue Number: 96-084324

ISBN: 0-9651855-0-8

Manufactured in the United States of America

First Printing: 1996

Book Design by

David Malone

To my mother,
who is the ultimate "Champagne Lady,"
and my family, all of whom have been so supportive
during the writing of this book.

Special Champagne wishes to
LeRoy Neiman,
who captures the true essence of Champagne
and allowed me to share his Art.

Contents

Acknowledgements

To a really special and unique group of friends, all of whom

have contributed to Champagne . . . Uncorked!!!

Robin Leach, CIVC and Jean-Louis Carbonnier,

Tony and Lisa Damiano, Tschida and Thomas Gruenebaum,

Usha and Bob Cunningham, Chris and Max Ansbacker,

Nicky and Jackie Drexel, Millicent Hearst Boudjakdji,

Vale and Ed Elkins, Josette and Aldo Donetto, Margo Hofeldt,

Lisa Renstron and Betty Anderson, Dee Sexton, Catherine Saxton, Jan Roberts

Foreword

For a decade, I've been encouraging everyone to receive with open arms the fine luxuries of life, one of the most essential pleasures being great Champagne. I would have to look far and wide for a more elegant, festive, decadent, and, yes, even sexy way to enjoy the good life than with a bottle—or more—of the bubbly. Now comes Rosemary's charming book that gets it all right so you don't go wrong. It's a must for anybody wanting to brighten up their life. Cheers, and Champagne Wishes, of course!

–Robin Leach, Host and Executive Producer of
"Lifestyles of the Rich and Famous"

Rosemary
at table
Le Cirque with love
LeRoy Neiman

16
30
95

Preface

No other wine so instantly contributes such an air of festivity and gaiety as Champagne. Champagne is unique and very special because it makes us feel special.

I feel very privileged to have spent the past twelve years representing various Champagne houses and to have worked with so many marvelous and stimulating people.

So I raise my glass with much love to all my Champagne friends in France and America and with a toast to all Champagne lovers for good health and happiness.

—The Champagne Lady

Winston Churchill said of Champagne:

"In Success you deserve it and in Defeat, you need it."

Born in Bubbles

The Place...
The Grapes...
The 12 Months
of Champagne

LeRoy Neiman

What Is This Magic Called Champagne?

Champagne is Champagne only when it comes from grapes grown in the Champagne area in France. Bubbles have to be born in Champagne to inherit the name Champagne; everything else is sparkling wine, whether it grows up in California, Germany, Spain, or even France.

"By Any Other Name"

Champagne, then, is unique and everything else is sparkling wine. That does not mean that sparkling wines are inferior; it simply means that they have a different personality and style. Many French Champagne houses have, in fact, purchased land and are producing sparkling wines in California. Even though the child is growing up in California, the style of its French parents is still perceptible in the taste.

Unique

The Place

Champagne, in northeast France, is the most northerly of all French wine-growing areas. To protect the quality of the wine, French law in 1927 precisely defined the Champagne area. It is composed of large and small plots comprising 35,000 hectares. Chalk is characteristic of the soil of all Champagne vineyards and ensures excellent drainage and moisture for the vines. Chalk absorbs and retains the sun's heat, which is necessary to ripen the grapes, and adds the minerals which give the grapes their unique character and taste.

The Champagne area is divided into four main regions. The Montagne de Reims area represents 28 percent of the region and produces Pinot Noir and Pinot Meunier. The valley of the Marne represents 35 percent of the region and produces mainly Pinot Meunier. The Côte des Blancs, south of Epernay, owes its name to the Chardonnay grape and represents 12 percent of the region. Aube represents 25 percent of the region and produces Pinot Noir.

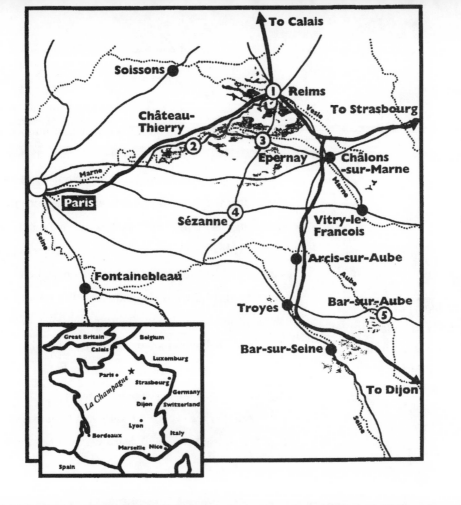

Bubbles

As he was opening a bottle of Champagne last summer, scientist Bill Lembeck speculated on how many bubbles would soon come bursting to life. Having realized that there would probably not be the same number of bubbles in every bottle, Bill Lembeck decided that he would be satisfied with a reasonable estimate. He then determined that essentially all he had to do was calculate the volume of CO_2 in a 750 ml bottle of Champagne and divide this number by the volume of an average bubble. Putting aside such questions as whether all the bubbles are the same size, and what is the impact of temperature on the size of the escaping bubble, Lembeck doggedly attacked the problem in a systematic way. First, he established that the average pressure in a Champagne bottle was about 5.5 atmospheres at 20 degrees C. In other words, he

How do bubbles get into Champagne? They develop naturally from a second fermentation inside the tightly corked bottle.

explained, a bottle of Champagne contains 5.5 times its volume in the form of gas produced by the second fermentation in the bottle. Accordingly (at standard atmospheric pressure), a 750 ml bottle contains 4,125 ml (252 cubic inches) of gas dissolved in the wine. The gas is not released until the cork is removed. The next step in Lembeck's scientific inquiry was to determine the size and volume of an average Champagne bubble. With the aid of a machine called an "optical comparitor," Lembeck was able to determine the average bubble diameter at the surface of the wine in a glass. It was 0.5 mm (0.020 in.). Knowing this, it was child's play for him to compute the volume of the average bubble: a minuscule 69 millionths of a ml (4.2 millionths of a cubic inch). A non-scientist would hastily have concluded that all that remained was to divide the total volume of gas by the volume of an average bubble. Lembeck, being a scientist, knew that at least one 750 ml volume of the CO_2 dissolved in the liquid would remain behind when the cork was removed: 750 ml of CO_2 that would never burst. The available CO_2 would therefore be the originally calculated CO_2 (4,125 ml) minus the trapped CO_2 (750 ml), leaving 3,375 ml (206 cubic inches) destined for bubbledom. Finally, all that remained for Lembeck to do was divide this available volume of gas by that of the average bubble. He obtained the astonishing number of 49 million bubbles per bottle. Believe it or not.

–Adapted with permission from an article by Bill Lembeck

The Grapes

Champagne is produced from three different grapes—the
Chardonnay, Pinot Noir, and Pinot Meunier.
The white Chardonnay
gives the wine elegance and finesse; the black
Pinot Noir gives it character, body, and depth; the
black Pinot Meunier blends the tastes and helps younger
wines taste older. Although Champagne is made from two-thirds
black grapes, the result is a white wine.

Champagne Types

MULTIVINTAGE (also known as non-vintage) Champagnes are the most popular, expressing the style of the Houses that make them. They are often called the "bread and butter" wines, as they represent approximately 90 percent of House production. In most Houses, multivintage is Brut (dry). The artistry of the Chef de Cave (wine-maker) comes in consistency of standard and style, from year to year.

You can open a quality bottle of Champagne anywhere in the world and it will taste the same. This is truly the art of the wine-maker. **ROSÉ** was created for Romance. There are two ways to make a Rosé Champagne. The first is by leaving the skins of the black grapes in contact with the "must" (unfermented grape juice) for a short period of time. The second is by adding a small amount of Bouzy red still wine to the Champagne before the second fermentation. Some Houses prefer this second method, as it allows them to keep the color more consistent.

Vintage Champagne is declared only in exceptional years. The wine must be made entirely from the year stated on the label. Many wine-makers believe that multivintage Champagne is their own art, while for the Vintage, they have to share the credit with God! Every House has the right to decide for itself whether the incoming year will be declared a vintage.

Champagne Prestige wines (Cuvée) are the crème de la crème and are made from the finest grapes and the finest vineyards. **Deluxe Cuvées**, as they are sometimes called, should be treated as a "reward for achievement." Even in Champagne families, who could easily afford to drink their top Champagnes every day, these wines are reserved for special occasions, such as a child's graduation, engagement, or wedding, a promotion, or winning a horse race.

The Twelve Months of Champagne

SEPTEMBER . . . THE HARVEST

Champagne takes one year of hard labor before the growers can harvest the grapes; it takes three years before the wine ends up in your glass. The grapes in Champagne are picked by hand.

OCTOBER . . . THE PRESSING

After the Champagne grapes are picked, they are put in for pressing or taken to a press house right in the vineyard. The grapes are pressed very quickly; four hours' work yields 2,550 liters of Champagne wines per 4,000 kilos of grapes. The wine is then transferred to stainless steel tanks, where the must is fermented. (A very few Houses still ferment in oak barrels, but most use stainless steel.) The wine is racked several times to get rid of the sediments.

NOVEMBER . . . THE TILLING OF THE SOIL

The vines are readied for a cold winter as the soil is gently pushed against the root stock to give better insulation.

DECEMBER . . . THE BOTTLING—TASTING BEGINS

The rain and snow wash the soil down the stiff slopes of the vines. It is then necessary to carry the soil back and add a fresh supply each year. Strict rules govern this procedure in the Champagne region.

When the cuvée blend has been achieved, the wine of the year is bottled and begins its long journey, which transforms the wine into Champagne.

JANUARY . . . THE FERMENTATION

The bottled wine is laid on racks to rest. The second fermentation produces carbon dioxide; the "prise de mousse" causes the wine to sparkle. Then it ages quietly until it is disgorged.

Fermentation

FEBRUARY . . . THE RIDDLING

In the cellars, the wine that is two to three years old is given a gentle twist, which causes the sediment to slide slowly down into the neck of the bottle, before the Champagne can be disgorged and shipped. The process is called "riddling." However, some prestige cuvées are still done by hand by the "remueur" and most Houses today have mechanical riddling, which is faster and more economical.

MARCH . . . THE PRUNING

If there is no frost, the vine plant is cut very short to limit production and improve the quality of the grapes.

APRIL . . . THE BUDDING

The wine-growers watch out for the unforeseeable and dreadful spring frosts, which are extremely destructive to the vine. Soon buds begin to appear on the vines.

MAY . . . DISGORGING

During this time, the vines have grown and spread out; they must be tied to the wires. Some wine-growers still flatten out the soil to aerate the topsoil.

In the great Champagne Houses, the disgorging sites are set up. The capped bottle is placed in a freezing brine solution, so that ice pellets form in the neck of the bottle. They retain the deposit; once the cap is removed, the deposit shoots out and is replaced with a "dosage." (Each brand has a special formula, but it is uniformly cane sugar and wine.) The bottle is then corked and the bottling process is finished.

In the early days, every bottle was disgorged by hand, just as every bottle was riddled by hand. This process is still used in several Champagne Houses. It requires a good flick of the wrist to get rid of the sediment without wasting any wine from the bottle.

Disgorging

Flowering

JUNE . . . THE FLOWERING

Toward the middle of June, the vines begin to flower. Wine-growers lower the wires; otherwise, the young vine-shoots will never be able to cling to the wires. At the same time, they nip numerous buds in order to limit production. The grapes are beginning to form, after natural pollination, during the months of June and July. The wine-growers keep an anxious eye on the weather.

JULY . . . THE SETTING OF THE GRAPES

The wine-growers thin out the leaves to help the grapes catch the full warmth of the sun. Grapes slowly mature under the sun and await a plentiful harvest. Needless to say, the wine-growers do not want too much rain during this period.

AUGUST . . . THE SHIPPING

After a minimum two to three years in the
cellars, shipment begins all over the world.

SEPTEMBER . . . THE HARVEST

And so the cycle is complete. Once again,
September brings another year's harvest,
about 100 days after flowering.

Harvest

The Makeup of a Bottle's Cost

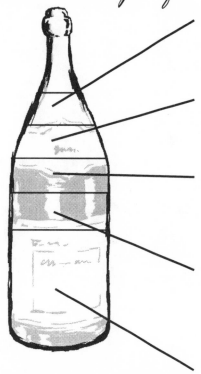

shipping

aging, disgorging, labeling, corks

cellaring, blending, bottling, stocks

labor: hand picking, pressing, handling, and other wine-making

grapes (1.2 kg/bottle)

A famous Englishman on his deathbed:

"My only regret is that I did not drink more Champagne."

Lord Maynard Keynes

Taste Will Tell

Styles...Conducting a
Tasting...Reading
the Label

TOP
OF THE
MARK

LeRoy Neiman

Champagne Styles and "Split" Personalities

Those of us who first met inexpensive sparkling wines at wedding receptions may have the mistaken idea that they all taste alike. When you taste five different Champagnes from one house, however, you begin to see that Champagne has many different personalities and styles. The styles are referred to as light-bodied, medium-bodied, and full-bodied. A light-bodied style could be described as being like Grace Kelly—elegant and refined, with great finesse. A full-bodied style could be described as Marilyn Monroe: it's all up front.

Styles

The Family Tree

Champagne Houses are like families. They have a Mother and Father who have created the "family style." They each have a number of children, such as multivintage, vintage, and so forth, which have a distinct personality but maintain the overall style of the family. Most Champagne Houses have one style or the other, and if you don't like that particular style, you try another House. A very few Houses make several styles within the same family.

Family

The Children

One House, for example, has a family style of light-bodied to medium-bodied, with emphasis on the Chardonnay grape. The "children" of that House are

Multivintage: 60% Chardonnay, 35% Pinot Noir, 5% Pinot Meunier

Rosé: 60% Pinot Noir, 40% Pinot Meunier

Vintage: 60% Pinot Noir, 35% Chardonnay, 5% Pinot Meunier

Blanc de Blancs/Vintage: 100% Chardonnay

Rosé/Vintage: 100% Pinot Noir

"Must" Knows

Family style shows through in the taste, but each of the "children" has a different personality. Part of the difference in personality is due to the combination of grapes and part is due to the grading of the must. "Must" is the name for the juice that comes from pressing the grapes. The first pressing, which is the best juice, is called "cuvée" and is limited to 2,050 liters. A few Champagne Houses use only the first pressing for their Champagnes. The second pressing, or taille, is vatted separately from the cuvée. The process usually takes three to four hours, and the grapes will have produced two very separate and distinct qualities and quantities of must.

Taste Will Tell

The best way to distinguish between styles and personalities and to develop a memory is to conduct informal tastings. However, there is one caution. Champagne tastings are like a good relationship: enjoy and share, but try not to overanalyze what makes it work or you risk losing the essence.

The Millennium

The upcoming Millennium is expected to be the largest Champagne night in history. The year 2000 will be celebrated December 31, 1999, and it is projected that 354 million bottles will be consumed all over the world on that night alone. Try one of these five fabulous tastings. Plan early to make this a once-in-a-lifetime evening with your friends.

Conducting a Champagne Tasting

Whether you want a professional tasting or an at-home tasting, the following will give you some ideas. Once you have conducted several tastings, I'm sure you will come up with your own creative ideas.

First, you will need these formulas:

1 bottle of Champagne = 5 glasses (for by-the glass tasting)

1 case of Champagne = 60 glasses

1 bottle of Champagne = 15 tastes (for large groups of 15-30)

1 case of Champagne = 120 tastes

You should figure two glasses per person for a two-hour cocktail party.

Types of Tastings

The make-up of your group should determine the type of tasting you decide to conduct. If your audience knows very little about Champagne, I would suggest starting with a Multivintage Tasting.

Multivintage Tastings

Begin with three or four different multivintage Champagnes that represent different styles and different Houses. This will help each person determine what style of Champagne he or she prefers. Obviously, this will not happen overnight, and you will need to have several of these types of tastings. However, if you have a group of Champagne lovers, this will be accomplished sooner!

Multivintage Versus Vintage Tasting

Pick one or two Houses and conduct a tasting of the multivintages as compared to the vintages. This will help to educate the palate about differences in grape styles and how a particular year can influence the taste and style of a Champagne. Keep it limited in the beginning; once you consider yourself ready, then you can try additional Houses.

Taste

Rosé Tasting

Rosé is often referred to as the "red wine of Champagne." Just as with *blanc* (white) Champagnes, there are many different styles; the tasting can include either all multivintage or all vintage. Have fun with this one, and you will end up a Rosé lover.

Tête de Cuvée Tasting

This is the grandest of tastings and, of course, the most expensive. If you've had a great year, consider this tasting for New Year's Eve. What a way to start the New Year!

Champagne Dinner Tasting

After you have narrowed the field from your previous tastings and have decided on your favorites, it is time to experiment with different food matches. I have used this suggested Champagne Dinner Menu all over the world. Bon appétit!

Hors d'oeuvre
Multivintage Champagne

First Course—Fish (salmon, bass, trout)

Main Course—Lamb
Rosé Champagne

Salad with Cheese (with a non-vinegar dressing)

Dessert
Demi-Sec Champagne

Of course, there are no set rules as to what goes with what. Experiment, and above all, have fun!!! What a great way to start the year 2000.

What to Look for When Tasting Champagne

Hold the glass against a white background to see the color, which can range from pale straw to light golden tones.

Look for small, elegant bubbles. It has often been said that "Champagne speaks to you in its bubbles."

Smell the bouquet, which should be dry, clean, and fresh. Often the nose, which will have a flowery, fruity aroma, will be an indication of the taste.

Swirl the Champagne around your palate. A quality Champagne will have character, length (extension of flavor), and a lingering aftertaste on the palate. (Terms often used to describe Champagne include crisp, delicate, fruity, full, fragrant, clean, balanced, dry, fresh, sweet, and smooth.)

Look for a balance between the fruit and the acid in the wine; there should be no "acid bite."

The label on a bottle of Champagne is too often taken for granted.

For the *Champenois*, it is a way to communicate and to attract the attention of the buyer—a true vehicle of promotion and marketing, unique to *la Champagne*!

It was not until the middle of the eighteenth century that embryonic labels appeared in the region (and elsewhere, for that matter). They began as small bits of paper pasted on bottles with a few handwritten comments.

❶ CHAMPAGNE

❷ HENRI MARTIN

❸ *Brut*

❹ REIMS

❺ 12% Vol.   **❻ Produce of France**   **❼ 75 Cl.**

❽ N.M. 204-007   **❾ Élaboré par Henri Martin, 5100 Reims, France**

❿ IMPORTED BY FINE WINES CO., NY, NY

The first true *étiquettes*, similar to familiar modern labels, began to be used by Champagne Houses around 1820. Soon, producers vied to outdo one another in originality and imagination. As they developed labels for special events and personalities, the Champagne labels became mirrors of history and culture.

Reading a label, understanding the rules of étiquette

Today, the label is a consumer informant. For *Champenois* producers, the label is a flag; it tells the identity and origin of the wine. For consumers, it is a guide and a protection against fraudulent imitations.

The following must appear on all labels:

1. Appellation of Controlled Origin: Champagne—prominently displayed

2. Brand, *marque*—differentiates the wines of different producers

3. Degree of sweetness—extra-brut, driest wines; brut, very dry (most wines are brut); extra-dry, slightly sweet; sec, sweet; demi-sec, very sweet

4. Country of origin—France

5. Town—Reims/Epernay, where the wine was made

6. Alcohol content—varies between 10.5% and 13%; 11% is the minimum for vintage dated wines

7. Volume of bottle—in centiliters

8. Trade registration—each producer is given a registration number by CIVC (the trade organization

for Champagne wines). When the producer owns the brand, the following initials will be found:

NM—*négociant-manipulant*, shipper, a Champagne House

CM—*coopérative de manipulation*, a co-operative of growers

RM—*récoltant-manipulant*, a grower who independently produces Champagne wines with his or her own grapes

RC—*récoltant-coopérateur*, a grower who produces Champagne with the help of a co-operative

MA—*marque d'acheteur*, when the brand is owned by a third party who is not a producer

9. Wine-maker, *élaborateur*—Champagne House, grower, or co-operative responsible for making the wine. This indication is either spelled out or coded.

10. Name of the U.S. importer.

Other indications on the label are optional. They include:

Vintage year, *millésime*—if the wine is exclusively made from the grapes of one vintage.

Reference to the grape variety used: Blanc de blancs for Champagne wines from 100% Chardonnay grapes; *Blanc de noirs* from 100% Pinot Noir and/or Meunier grapes

Reference to the cru: *Grand Cru* or *Premier Cru* refer to the best-rated villages of *la Champagne*. There are 17 Grands Crus, including Ambonnay, Avize, Aÿ, Bouzy, Cramant, Le Mesnil-sur-Oger, Tours-sur-Marne, and 41 Premiers Crus, including Chouilly, Hautvillers, Mareuil-sur-Aÿ.

Champagne Houses by Wine Styles

Each producer takes pride in its distinctive House style and strives for a consistent blend year after year.

Although it is difficult to be precise, the Champagne experts believe the following list is generally accurate.

Light, delicate

Abelé, Batiste-Pertois, Besserat de Bellefon,
Bricout, Castellane, A. Charbaut et Fils,
Jacquesson, Lanson, Taillevent

Light to medium

Ayala, Billecart-Salmon, Deutz, Laurent-Perrier, G.H. Mumm,
Perrier-Jouët, Pommery, Ruinart, Taittinger, De Venoge, Nicolas Feuillatte

Styles

Medium

Charles Heidsieck, Delamotte, Jacquart, Moët et Chandon, Joseph Perrier, Philipponnat, Piper-Heidsieck, Pol Roger

Medium to full

Paul Bara, Heidsieck Monopole, Henriot, Louis Roederer, Salon, J. Sélosse

Full, rich

Bollinger, Drappier, Gosset, Alfred Gratien, Krug, Veuve Clicquot

Vintage Chart
1982-1995

Harvest	Start	Production†	Comments	Vintage or MILLESIME
1995	Sept. 18	1,046,500	Good to very good quality. Late flowering due to a cool and humid spring. Exceptionally hot summer ended with rainfalls. Abundant grapes were severely selected and more often than not only first pressings were kept.	†††
1994	Sept. 15	890,000 *Blocage††: 51,000* Yield: 60 hl/ha	Good quality for blending. Very propitious flowering and wonderful summer. Rain set in a few days before harvest. Severe selection of the grapes at picking time and careful pressing permitted obtaining satisfactory musts.	†††
1993	Sept. 8	939,000 *Blocage: 180,000*	Satisfactory quality for multi-vintage blending. Fair winter and mild spring. Early September rainfall led to selective picking of the grapes and careful pressing.	†††

Vintage Chart

1982-1995

Harvest	Start	Production†	Comments	Vintage or *MILLESIME*
1992	Sept. 14	1,051,000 *Blocage:* 249,000	Good quality for the blending of multi-vintage wines. Late bud-break, hot May, early mid-June flowering. Rainy summer. Definitive elimination of *seconde taille*/third pressing.	†††
1991	Sept. 30	1,018,000	Fine quality. April frost, end of June flowering and propitious weather until mid-September.	†††
1990	Sept. 11	1,071,000	Extraordinary year in quality and quantity. Damaging spring frost followed by overall warm weather conditions.	***** 9/10
1989	Sept. 4	1,023,000	Spectacular quality. Severe frost in April and unusually early flowering. Extraordinary good weather and exceptional maturity. Rare second harvest in October.	***** 9/10

Vintage Chart
1982-1995

Harvest	Start	Production†	Comments	Vintage or *MILLESIME*
1988	Sept. 26	822,000	Very good quality. Mild and rainy winter. Spring frost and rainy May. Dry and stormy summer. First implementation of flexible picking "start-dates" through the 312 crus.	**** 8/10
1987	Sept. 28	969,000	Straightforward and clean wines for classic multi-vintage blending. Rainy year. Late flowering in early July. September's Indian summer saved the harvest.	6/10 Seldom Declared
1986	Sept. 28	957,000 *Blocage:* *103,000*	Good quality. Very late bud break end of April/early May. Cold spring and exceptionally rapid flowering at the end of June.	*** 7/10
1985	Sept. 30	560,000	Excellent quality in small quantity. Extremely severe frost in January and at the end of April. Superb sunny weather in September and October.	***** 9/10

Vintage Chart

1982-1995

Harvest	Start	Production†	Comments	Vintage or *MILLESIME*	
1984	Oct. 10	725,000	Disappointing year. Cool weather in June, poor summer and rainy fall.	Not Declared	
1983	Sept. 26	1,100,000 *Blocage: 280,000*	Powerful wines of superb quality. Largest harvest ever. Poor spring. Beautiful weather in summer and early autumn.	****	8/10
1982	Sept. 17	1,080,000 *Blocage: 89,000*	Rich voluptuous wines to drink now. Cool but frost-free winter. Warm summer and sunny September.	****	8/10

Vintage Chart
1982-1995

†*pièces*: Champenois cask, equivalent to about 55 gallons.
††*blocage*: Reserve of still wine which cannot be traded immediately, but is used to supplement poor or deficient harvests.
†††Because it takes three to five years between the time of harvest and market availability, the vintage is not known.
***** Exceptional **** Very Good *** Good

Older vintages of special importance to Champagne lovers:

1979: classic vintage****; 1976: rich powerful wines*****; 1975: stylish****; 1973: elegant wines****; 1971: firm wines with much finesse****; 1969: classic vintage****; 1966: delicious vintage*****; 1964: remarkable****; 1962: excellent wines****; 1961: great finesse****; 1959: exceptional wines*****

Collector's vintages of the greatest quality include:
1955, 1953, 1952, 1949, 1947, 1945, 1943, 1921, 1919, 1914, 1911

Markets

These were the top ten Champagne markets in 1996 (figures are given in millions of bottles).

1. France	160.0	6. Italy	7.3
2. Germany	17.7	7. Belgium	6.4
3. England	16.9	8. Netherlands	1.9
4. U.S.A.	12.0	9. Japan	1.8
5. Switzerland	7.4	10. Spain	1.2

Bigger Is Better

No one seems to know when, how or where these
titles were given to these large over-sized bottles. The following
gives you a brief description of each bottle.

Size	Total Bottles	Liters & Milliliters	Ounces
Split	1/4	187 ml	6.3 oz.
Half Bottle	1/2	375 ml	12.7 oz.
Bottle	1	750 ml	25.4 oz.
Magnum	2	1.5 liters	50.7 oz.
Jeroboam	4	3.0 liters	101.4 oz.
Rehoboam	6	4.5 liters	156.0 oz.
Methuselah	8	6.0 liters	202.8 oz.
Salmanazar	12	9.0 liters	307.2 oz.
Balthazar	16	12 liters	416.0 oz.
Nebuchadnezzar	20	15 liters	520.0 oz.
Sovereign	36	27 liters	936.0 oz.

The feeling of friendship
is like that of being comfortably filled with roast beef;
love is like being enlivened with Champagne.

Samuel Johnson

Champagne, Oyster and Corn Soup

This recipe was provided by Anne Rosensweig, chef/owner of Arcadia/Lobster Box, New York, New York.

5 ears of corn
30 oysters
$^1/_4$ cup light olive oil
4 large shallots, peeled, minced
1 teaspoon minced garlic
1 potato, peeled, finely chopped

$^3/_4$ cup Champagne
4 cups chicken or fish stock
1 cup cream
Salt and pepper to taste
$^1/_4$ cup chopped parsley

Champagne and Chefs

Cooking With
Champagne: Recipes For
Everyday Meals From
Acclaimed Chefs

Shelby Neiman

co-owner
Chef Rosenzweig

huck the corn; remove the kernels from the cobs with a sharp knife. Shell the oysters and drain them, reserving the liquor. Combine the olive oil and shallots in a large sauté pan. Cook over medium-high heat until the shallots are translucent. Add the garlic and potato. Cook for 2 minutes, stirring constantly. Add the Champagne. Cook for 1 minute. Stir in the corn, reserved oyster liquor and chicken stock. Bring to a boil and cook for 7 minutes. Stir in the cream and heat thoroughly. Add the oysters. Cook until the edges of the oysters have curled. Season with the salt and pepper. Stir in the parsley and serve immediately.

Yields 4 to 6 servings.

Champagne-Pineapple Clove Ice

This recipe and the next were provided by Stephen Pyles, chef/owner of Star Canyon, Dallas, Texas.

$1/3$ cup whole cloves
$1^1/_2$ cups Champagne
1 medium pineapple, peeled, cored, chopped
Juice of 1 lemon
1 cup Simple Syrup

Bring the cloves and Champagne to a boil in a medium saucepan; reduce the heat. Simmer for 5 minutes; remove from the heat. Let stand for 4 hours or longer to infuse. Strain the mixture into a large bowl, discarding the cloves. Purée the pineapple in a blender or food processor. Press through a fine strainer into the Champagne mixture. Add the lemon juice and Simple Syrup and mix well. Pour the mixture into an ice cream freezer container. Freeze using the manufacturer's directions.

Yields 1 quart.

Simple Syrup

This mixture is a foundation for making all types of ices; it keeps indefinitely in the refrigerator.

3 cups sugar
2¹/₂ cups water

Combine the sugar and water in a large saucepan. Cook over high heat for 3 to 4 minutes or until the sugar dissolves, stirring constantly with a wooden spoon. Bring to a full boil; remove from the heat. Set aside to cool completely. Refrigerate in an airtight container.

Yields 1 quart.

"A toast of Champagne has always epitomized camaraderie, celebration, and success. One taste of its crisp, fruitful effervescence can invoke the most festive of moments."

Stephen Pyles

Oysters in Champagne Sauce

This recipe was provided by Andrew d'Amico, Executive Chef at Sign of the Dove, New York, New York.

6 ounces Champagne
2 tablespoons minced shallots
1 cup whipping cream
6 tablespoons butter, softened

18 oysters, shelled
1/4 cup chervil leaves or chopped parsley
Salt and freshly ground pepper to taste

*C*ombine the Champagne and shallots in a 2-quart saucepan. Cook until the liquid is reduced by one-half. Whisk in the whipping cream. Cook until reduced by one-fourth. Whisk in the butter 1 tablespoon at a time. Add the oysters and chervil. Simmer until the oysters are heated through. Season with the salt and pepper. Arrange oysters on 6 individual serving plates. Spoon a small amount of the Champagne sauce over each oyster. Garnish with caviar.

Yields 6 servings.

"Just watching the tiny bubbles of Champagne rise up through a glass puts most people in a festive mood. Wonderful food and great Champagne are the perfect evening!"

Andrew d'Amico

Champagne Rollos de Lenguado (Fillet of Flounder)

This recipe was provided by Josephina Howard, chef/owner of Rosa Mexicano, New York, New York.

8 poblano chiles, roasted, peeled, deveined

Salt to taste

8 flounder fillets

Pepper to taste

Fresh lemon juice to taste

1 small onion, finely chopped

1 small tomato, finely chopped

1 clove of garlic, finely chopped

2 tablespoons butter

6 ounces baby shrimp, finely chopped

4 ounces bay scallops, finely chopped

4 cups fish stock

Vegetable oil for sautéing

$\frac{1}{2}$ cup chicken stock

1 cup whipping cream

1 cup Champagne

oak the chiles in hot salted water for 1 hour. Pound the fillets between sheets of waxed paper to flatten them slightly. Season with the salt and pepper. Sprinkle with the lemon juice and set aside. Reserve a small amount of the onion for the sauce. Sauté the remaining onion, tomato and garlic in the butter in a sauté pan. Add the shrimp and scallops. Sauté for 5 minutes. Spoon the mixture into the fillets; roll up the fillets and secure with wooden picks. Use a slotted spoon to drop the rolls into simmering fish stock in a large saucepan. Cook for 5 minutes. Drain the chiles and cut them into strips. Sauté the chiles and the reserved onion in a small amount of oil in a skillet. Combine with the chicken stock in a blender container. Process until of paste consistency. Heat the whipping cream in a small saucepan until it is reduced by one-half. Stir in the chile paste. Strain into a large saucepan. Add the Champagne. Cook until heated through; do not boil. Arrange the rollos on individual serving plates and spoon the Champagne sauce over them.

Yields 4 servings.

Scallops of Striped Bass with Tomato

This recipe was provided by Piero Selvaggio, chef/owner of Valentino, Los Angeles, California.

1 (3-pound) striped bass
2 quarts water
1 clove of garlic, chopped
1 scallion, chopped
1 stalk celery, chopped
2 tomatoes, peeled, chopped
1 carrot, chopped
1 bay leaf

$^{1}/_{2}$ cup (about) flour
3 tablespoons olive oil
1 clove of garlic, crushed
$^{1}/_{3}$ cup dry Champagne
$^{1}/_{4}$ cup Brandy
1 teaspoon Worcestershire sauce
2 tomatoes, peeled, chopped
$^{1}/_{2}$ cup unsalted butter

emove the scales and head from the fish and place them in a large saucepan, reserving the fish. Add the water, chopped garlic, scallion, celery, 2 tomatoes, carrot and bay leaf to the saucepan. Bring to a boil and reduce the heat. Simmer for 1 hour, skimming the top occasionally. Strain the stock through a cheesecloth and set it aside. Cut the fish into 6 steaks and coat thoroughly with the flour. Heat the olive oil in a large skillet over medium-high heat. Add the crushed garlic and the fish steaks. Sauté for 1 minute per side. Add the Champagne and Brandy and flambé them. Remove the fish steaks to a covered dish; set them aside and keep them warm. Add the Worcestershire sauce, remaining 2 tomatoes and butter to the cooking liquid in the skillet. Cook over medium-high heat for 1 to 2 minutes or until the liquid is reduced by one-half, stirring constantly. Place the fish steaks on individual serving plates. Spoon the sauce over the top. Garnish each serving with a fresh basil leaf.

Yields 6 servings.

"Champagne is a special wine. The special occasion wine may be to liven up our days, raise to a special moment, or stop and sip the magic of great wine-making. For me, it is excellent to drink at any time, all through a meal, all the time."

Piero Selvaggio

Chilled Strawberry Soup with Champagne and Saffron

This recipe was provided by Kevin Garvin, Vice President of Food Service, Neiman Marcus, Dallas, Texas.

2 pints fresh strawberries
1 quart Champagne
$1/2$ cup sugar
1 orange, channeled, sliced
1 lemon, channeled, sliced
1 bay leaf
1 sprig of fresh thyme
$1/10$ teaspoon saffron
16 fresh mint leaves

ash the strawberries and remove the stems, reserving 8 strawberries for a garnish. Combine the remaining strawberries, Champagne, sugar, orange slices, lemon slices, bay leaf, thyme and saffron in a saucepan. Bring to a boil; reduce the heat. Simmer for 20 to 30 minutes or until the sugar is dissolved and the mixture is heated through. Pour into a chilled bowl and let stand until cool. Remove and discard the orange slices, lemon slices, bay leaf and thyme. Purée the mixture in a food processor. Filter through a fine colander or sieve into a bowl. Chill, covered, for 6 hours. Ladle the soup into chilled individual bowls. Cut the reserved strawberries into quarters. Arrange 4 strawberry pieces and 2 mint leaves on top of each bowl of soup.

Yields 8 servings.

"Champagne is the ultimate special occasion wine, but I hate to limit it like that. A glass of Champagne is the perfect apéritif—and a great finish to any meal."

Kevin Garvin

Pizza with Smoked Salmon and Caviar

This recipe and the next were provided by Wolfgang Puck, chef/owner of Spago Restaurant, Los Angeles, California.

1 recipe Pizza Dough (page 74)
$^1/_4$ cup extra-virgin olive oil
$^1/_2$ medium red onion, cut into julienne strips
$^1/_4$ bunch fresh dill, minced
$^1/_3$ cup sour cream or crème fraîche

Freshly ground pepper to taste
3 to 4 ounces smoked salmon, cut into paper-thin slices
$^1/_4$ cup (heaping) domestic golden caviar
1 teaspoon (heaping) black caviar

lace a pizza stone in the oven. Preheat to 500 degrees for 30 minutes. Roll or stretch the pizza dough into four 8-inch circles. Place the pizzas on a lightly floured wooden surface. Brush the center of each pizza to within 1 inch of the edge with olive oil; sprinkle with some of the onion. Slide 1 pizza onto the stone. Bake for 8 to 12 minutes or until the crust is golden brown. Bake the remaining pizzas in the same fashion. Transfer the pizzas to heated dinner plates. Mix the dill, sour cream and pepper in a bowl. Spread over the pizzas. Arrange the salmon over the sour cream mixture. Place a spoonful of golden caviar in the center of each pizza. Spoon a small amount of the black caviar into the center of the golden caviar.

Yields 4 pizzas.

Pizza Dough

Wolfgang Puck is justifiably noted for his pizzas.

1 package active dry or fresh yeast

1 teaspoon honey or sugar

$1/4$ cup warm (105 to 115 degrees) water

$2^3/4$ cups flour

1 teaspoon salt

2 tablespoons olive oil

$1/2$ cup warm (105 to 115 degrees) water

*D*issolve the yeast and honey in $^1/_4$ cup water in a small bowl; set aside. Combine the flour and salt in a mixer bowl, fitted with a dough hook. Add the oil, stirring until all the liquid is absorbed. Stir in the yeast mixture. Add the remaining $^1/_2$ cup water. Knead at low speed for 5 minutes. Turn out onto a floured board. Knead for 2 to 3 minutes longer or until the dough is smooth and firm. Cover with a damp towel and let rise in a warm place for 30 minutes or until the dough stretches when lightly pulled. Divide the dough into 4 balls. Work each ball by pulling down the sides and tucking under the bottom of the ball; repeat 4 or 5 times. Place 1 ball on a smooth unfloured surface. Roll under the palm of your hand for 1 minute or until the dough is smooth and firm. Repeat the process with the remaining dough. Let rest, covered with a damp towel, for 15 to 20 minutes. At this point, the balls can be loosely covered with plastic wrap and refrigerated for 1 to 2 days.

Yields 4 (7- to 8-inch) pizzas.

Rich-and-Famous Chicken

This recipe and the next were provided by Robin Leach,
"Lifestyles of the Rich and Famous."

3 tablespoons unsalted
butter
3 tablespoons flour
2 cups Essence of Silver
and Gold (page 78)
Salt and freshly ground
pepper to taste
2 large onions, sliced
2¹/₂ tablespoons unsalted
butter, thinly sliced
1 (3¹/₂- to 5-pound)
chicken, cut into 8
pieces

2 tablespoons Champagne
¹/₄ cup finely chopped fresh
basil leaves, or
2 tablespoons dried
2 tablespoons finely
chopped fresh oregano,
or 1 tablespoon dried
¹/₂ teaspoon dry mustard
1 tablespoon freshly
squeezed lemon juice
2 teaspoons steak sauce
¹/₂ pound white
mushrooms, trimmed,

wiped clean, thinly
sliced
1 pound carrots, trimmed,
peeled, cut into 1-inch
pieces
1 cup green peas
2¹/₂ tablespoons unsalted
butter, thinly sliced
³/₄ cup plus 2 tablespoons
Champagne
4 potatoes, peeled, cut into
¹/₂-inch cubes
1 cup whipping cream

*M*elt the 3 tablespoons butter in a heavy medium saucepan over medium-high heat. Stir in the flour; reduce the heat. Cook for 3 to 5 minutes or until well blended, whisking constantly. Stir in the Essence of Silver and Gold. Bring to a boil; reduce the heat. Simmer for 7 to 10 minutes or until thickened and smooth, stirring frequently. Season with salt and pepper. Remove from the heat and keep warm. Place the onions in a baking dish and dot with $2^{1}/_{2}$ tablespoons butter. Rinse the chicken and pat dry. Season with salt and pepper. Place the chicken on the onions. Sprinkle with 2 tablespoons Champagne, basil, oregano, mustard, lemon juice and steak sauce. Arrange the mushrooms, carrots and peas over the chicken. Top with the remaining butter. Sprinkle with 2 tablespoons Champagne. Pour the sauce over the chicken. Sprinkle with the remaining Champagne. Sink the potato cubes in the sauce, leaving only slightly submerged. Bake, tightly covered, at 425 degrees for 45 to 50 minutes or until the vegetables are tender and the chicken is cooked through. Bake, uncovered, for 10 minutes longer or until the potatoes are lightly browned. Arrange the chicken and vegetables on a serving platter and cover to keep warm. Bring the cream to a boil in a medium saucepan over high heat. Boil for 3 to 5 minutes or until reduced by one-half. Add to the pan juices. Boil for several minutes to reduce and thicken slightly. Pour over the chicken and serve immediately. This recipe may be prepared in a "romertopf," a clay pot designed for kitchen use; consult a clay pot cookbook for cooking times and temperatures.

Yields 4 to 6 servings.

Essence of Silver and Gold

Use your very best wine for this sauce;
compliments will be forthcoming.

2 (1-pound) pieces bottom round of veal, boned, tied

2 whole (1-pound) chicken breasts with bone

4 pounds veal bones

2 leeks, trimmed, rinsed, coarsely chopped

2 celery stalks, thickly sliced

2 medium carrots, thickly sliced

3 to 4 sprigs of fresh thyme, or 2 teaspoons dried

2 bay leaves

2 large onions, studded with 2 whole cloves

2 teaspoons salt

20 whole black peppercorns

12 cups water

4 cups dry white wine

*T*rim any fat from the veal and the chicken. Have the butcher saw the veal bones into 3 to 4 large pieces. Combine all the ingredients in a large nonreactive stockpot. Bring to a boil over medium-high heat; reduce the heat to medium. Simmer for 2 to 3 hours or until the liquid measures approximately 4 cups, skimming the top occasionally. Line a large sieve or colander with a double layer of cheesecloth or coarse muslin and set it inside a large bowl. Ladle the hot stock in carefully, discarding the solids. Cool to room temperature. Cover and chill in the refrigerator. Remove any fat that hardens on the top.

Yields 4 cups.

Roasted Sea Bass with Champagne Sauce, Haricots Verts and Carrots

This recipe was provided by Sylvain Portay, Le Cirque Restaurant, New York, New York.

1/2 pound green beans

1/2 pound carrots, sliced diagonally

2 tablespoons butter

1 head of garlic

2 shallots

1/2 bottle Champagne

1/2 cup plus 2 tablespoons butter

4 (6-ounce) sea bass fillets

1 cup olive oil

2 cups whipping cream

Salt and pepper to taste

*B*lanch the green beans in boiling water in a saucepan and set aside. Combine the carrots, 2 tablespoons butter, garlic and a small amount of water in a saucepan. Cook until the carrots are tender. Sweat the shallots in a skillet. Deglaze with $^3/_4$ of the Champagne. Cook until the liquid is almost completely reduced. Stir in the remaining butter. Cook the fish in the olive oil in a hot skillet until tender. Arrange the carrots and green beans on the plate. Top with the fish. Fold enough of the whipping cream and the remaining Champagne into the sauce to create a foaming sauce. Place the garlic on the plate and arrange the sauce around it. Season with salt and pepper. Serve very hot.

Yields 4 servings.

The Champagne Lady's Chicken in Champagne Sauce with Green Peppercorns

6 tablespoons butter or margarine

12 chicken breasts, skinned, cut into small pieces

1/2 teaspoon salt

1 cup chicken broth

1 cup Champagne

12 medium to large mushrooms

8 tablespoons butter or margarine

6 tablespoons flour

2 cups half-and-half

1 teaspoon salt

1 teaspoon Dijon mustard

2 teaspoons green peppercorns

Champagne

$\mathcal{M}$ elt the 6 tablespoons butter in a roasting pan. Add the chicken, turning to coat the chicken on all sides. Arrange the chicken in a single layer in the pan. Sprinkle with the ¹/₂ teaspoon salt. Pour in the chicken broth and Champagne. Bake, tightly covered with foil, at 325 degrees for 40 minutes. Reserve 2 cups of the pan juices. Flute the mushroom caps. Melt 2 tablespoons of the remaining butter in a large skillet over low heat. Add the mushroom caps. Sauté for 2 minutes or until the mushrooms are browned and the juices flow freely. Chill until needed. Place the remaining 6 tablespoons butter in the skillet. Stir in the flour. Cook over medium heat for 2 minutes, stirring frequently. Add the half-and-half. Cook for 5 minutes or until thickened, stirring constantly. Stir in the reserved pan juices. Add the remaining 1 teaspoon salt, Dijon mustard and peppercorns. Bring to a boil. Pour the sauce over the chicken in the roasting pan. Bake, covered, at 325 degrees for 30 minutes or until heated through. Arrange the mushroom caps over the chicken. Bake, uncovered, for 5 minutes longer. Serve immediately.

Yields 8 to 10 servings.

Pour Champagne Wines

The Main Events	Summer Food Favorites
Rise 'n' Shine Summer Brunch	Egg dishes such as omelettes or frittatas.
	French toast, pancakes, crepes.
Sunday Breakfast	Sausage, bacon, smoked fish.
	Pastries, croissants, muffins, scones.
The Moveable Feast	Club sandwiches with turkey and ham.
	Deli-style submarine sandwiches.
Country Picnic	Fried chicken, potato salad, coleslaw.
Poolside Box Lunch	Cheese pizza with vegetables.
Beach Blanket Barbecue	Grilled vegetable sandwiches with mozzarella and pesto.
	Pasta and grain-based salads such as couscous, bulgur, lentil, orzo, rice. Seafood kabobs, burgers, ribs, corn on the cob.
Cocktails & Tea Time	Miniature puff pastries with seafood, cheese or vegetables.
	Quiche, egg roll, stuffed cherry tomatoes, crostini, tortillas and
Appetizer Buffet	salsa. Tomato and herb bruschetta. Finger sandwiches, assorted
Cocktails after Tennis	canapés.
Afternoon Tea	
Apéritif	

Into Your Summer

Dosage "Sweetness"	Styles of Wines	The Food & Champagne Experience
Brut	Vintage or Multivintage including Rosé and Blanc de Blancs	Best way to start the day. Bruts (very dry) open the appetite. Young Blanc de Blancs are especially refreshing while Rosés add festive notes of red berries.
Brut or Extra-Dry	Multivintage including Rosé	Multivintage Bruts and Extra-Drys are the most accessible Champagne wines. Acidity and effervescence bring relief and contrast to the simplest foods. Their quality creates excitement.
Brut or Extra-Dry	Multivintage including Blanc de Blancs	Champagne wines are convivial. They harmonize with a variety of flavors and cleanse the palate between morsels of food.

Pour Champagne Wines

The Main Events	Summer Food Favorites
Evening Magic . . . Dining Alfresco	Grilled meats and poultry such as shish kabobs, teriyaki steaks, pork chops, herb-marinated chicken. Stir-fry dishes with seafood, poultry and/or vegetables. Light or creamy pasta dishes such as linguini with white clam sauce, tortellini, fettuccini alfredo.
Patio Picnic	
Front Porch Supper with Neighbors	
Pre-Concert Picnic	
Star-Light Dining with Friends	
On the Lighter Side	Pasta dishes such as primaveras, linguini with fresh tomato, basil, and mozzarella. Pasta with pesto sauce. Grilled fish and seafood. Grilled garden vegetables with herbs. Take-out sushi, tempuras, and roasted chicken.
Cool & Breezy Dinners	
Midweek Get Together	
Time for Take-Out	
Late-Night Snacks	
Sweet Conclusions	Crème brûlée, mousse, flan, frozen yogurt, ice cream, Bavarian cream.
Delectable Desserts	
Summer's Bounty of Fresh Fruit	Berries solo or with shortcake, pound cake or biscotti. Fruit desserts such as pies, tarts, cobblers, crisps.

Into Your Summer

Dosage "Sweetness"	Styles of Wines	The Food & Champagne Experience
Brut or Extra-Dry	Vintage or Multivintage including Rosé and Blanc de Blancs	Bruts and Extra-Drys cut across the slightly fatty texture of fried foods. Light residual sweetness provides contrast to spicy, seasoned or peppery foods.
Brut	Vintage or Multivintage including Rosé and Blanc de Blancs	Champagne wines complement delicately flavored foods. Greater depth and complexity of aromas in vintage wines are well suited to grilled foods.
Extra-Dry, Sec or Demi-Sec	Multivintage	Higher residual sweetness in Extra-Dry, Sec and particularly Demi-Sec wines creates successful combinations with sweeter desserts.
Brut	Vintage or Multivintage including Rosé	Fresh fruit and bittersweet desserts are highlighted by Bruts. The natural notes of strawberry and raspberry in Rosé wines make them an ideal partner.

Pour Champagne Wines

The Main Events	Summer Food Favorites

Just Say Cheese

Cheeses for Dessert & Snacking

Brie, fresh goat cheese, Parmesan, Cheddar, Gruyère.

Stilton, Gorgonzola, double-crème.

Summer Celebrations

Romantic Dinner for Two
Garden Party Reception
Bon Voyage Party

Rack of lamb, duckling, broiled lobster, filet mignon.
Caviar, melon wrapped in prosciutto, smoked salmon.

Into Your Summer

Dosage "Sweetness"	Styles of Wines	The Food & Champagne Experience
Brut	Vintage or Multivintage including Rosé	Mature Bruts, Rosé especially, cut fattiness and saltiness in cheese. Acidity and complexity balance this exciting combination.
Extra-Dry, Sec or Demi-Sec	Multivintage	Sweeter wines complement the natural tangy flavors of creamy veined cheeses. Effervescence elevates and relieves.
Brut	Prestige cuvée, Vintage or Multivintage including Rosé and Blanc de Blancs	Prestige cuvées lend another dimension to special occasions: elegance, refinement, glory. Finesse and complexity contrast the rich flavors of special foods.

The Main Events

Winter Warming Starts

Weekend Breakfast
Chalet Brunch

The Moveable Feast

Tailgate Picnic
Fall Hayride
Football Game Box Lunch
Cross Country Ski Break

On The Lighter Side

Post Theatre Snacks
Bistro Supper
Take-out and a video

Fall & Winter Food Favorites

Eggs Florentine or Benedict, corned beef hash, home fries, hushpuppies, Belgian waffles, pancakes, French toast, bacon, sausage, smoked fish, blueberry blintzes, brioche, croissants, corn muffins.

Grilled steak sandwiches, meatball subs, vegetable pizza, pastrami on rye, gyro, hot dogs, French-fries, nachos, cheese snacks.

Baked potatoes, cream of asparagus soup, clam chowder, linguini carbonara, deep-dish pizza, steamed mussels, sushi, shrimp tempura, crispy noodles with beef, chicken fajitas.

With Champagne Wines

Dosage "Sweetness"	Styles of Wines	The Food & Champagne Experience
Brut	Multivintage, including Rosé, and Blanc de Blancs	The best way to start the day. Very dry Brut Champagnes whet the appetite. Light Blanc de Blancs are particularly appealing. Young Rosés add colorful and bright notes of red fruit.
Brut or Extra-Dry	Multivintage	Multivintage Bruts and Extra-Drys are widely available. Extra-Dry is a touch sweeter than Brut and complement foods with sweet or spicy flavors.
Brut	Vintage or Multivintage, including Rosé	Vintage wines have greater elegance, character and finesse. The acidity and effervescence of Champagne bring relief to the simplest foods. Its quality creates contrast and excitement.

Fall Into Winter

The Main Events

Joyful Affairs

Fireside Dining with Friends
Thanksgiving Dinner
Hanukkah Treats
Christmas Eve Supper

Cool Celebrations

Anniversary Téte-à-Téte
Winter Solstice Party
New Year's Eve Buffet

Romantic Escapes

Cruise to the Caribbean
Ski Lodge Retreat
Valentine's Day Country Inn

Fall & Winter Food Favorites

Honey-baked ham, crisp golden turkey, roast goose, sweet potato soufflé, yams, winter squash, potato pancakes, chestnut stuffing and gravy, Parmesan popovers, fig pudding.

Fresh oysters, caviar, broiled lobster tail, tiger shrimp, sautéed scallops, grilled quail, venison, veal roast, Cornish hen, truffles, roast monkfish, foie gras, wild rice.

Filet mignon, prime rib au jus, Peking duck, squab, blackened red snapper, salmon roe, roasted sea bass, seafood bisque, wild mushroom ravioli, penne in spinach sauce.

With Champagne Wines

Dosage "Sweetness"	Styles of Wines	The Food & Champagne Experience
Brut or Extra-Dry	Prestige cuvée, Vintage or Multivintage including Rosé and Blanc de Blancs	Champagne is the wine of conviviality and sharing. Prestige cuvées give an extra dimension to special occasions. They have the most character and complexity to balance the richness of celebration foods. Brut Rosés have more vinosity and fruit. They are also very festive. Blanc de Blancs are especially good with delicate foods.
Brut	Prestige cuvée, Vintage including Rosé	Champagne wines sparkle romance around the world. The mystique hides the quality and pleasure they bring to the table. Champagne provides an elegant counter point to elaborate foods. It also invigorates.

The Main Events	Fall & Winter Food Favorites
Conclusions	Apple tart, pumpkin pie, rhubarb crisp, mousse, poached pear, crème brûlée, Black Forest cake.
Delectable Desserts	
Cheese & Crackers	Jarlsburg, English farm Cheddar, Camembert, Parmesan, goat cheese.

With Champagne Wines

Dosage "Sweetness"	Styles of Wines	The Food & Champagne Experience
Extra-Dry, Sec or Demi-Sec	Multivintage	Successful combinations with desserts require wines sweeter than Brut.
Brut	Vintage or Multivintage, including Rosé	Mature Bruts, including Rosés, cut fat and saltiness in cheese. They also cleanse the palate and refresh.

When the late Lilly Bollinger was asked
by a London reporter when she drank Champagne, she replied:
"I drink it when I'm happy and when I'm sad.
Sometimes I drink it when I'm alone.
When I have company I consider it obligatory.
I trifle with it if I'm not hungry and drink when I am.
Otherwise I never touch it—unless I'm thirsty."

Morning, Noon & Night

The Champagne Cocktail
Cocktail Recipes

The Champagne Cocktail

In America, cocktails, which have virtually disappeared, are making a comeback. Dale DeGroff of New York's Rainbow Room says that the demand for Champagne-based cocktails has increased by 50 percent over the previous year. He is even doing seminars on cocktails and how to make them.

"Should I use Champagne or sparkling wine?" is usually the first question. The answer depends on personal preference and budget. For example, a world-renowned restaurateur famous for creating the Bellini would never think of using anything but Champagne in his Bellini cocktail. The Mimosa, probably the best known of the Champagne cocktails, can be made with either Champagne or sparkling wine. In Champagne, be it Reims or Epernay, you will see Champagne cocktails on every menu made, of course, with Champagne. Experiment with Champagne or sparkling wine in the following recipes.

The Original Champagne Cocktail

1 sugar cube
Angostura bitters
4 ounces chilled Champagne

Soak the sugar in the Angostura. Place the sugar cube in a Champagne flute. Fill with Champagne. Garnish with a twist of lemon.

The Champagne cocktail first appeared in print in 1862 in the first American cocktail book, "How to Mix Drinks, or The Bon-Vivant's Companion," by Jerry Thomas. The recipe remains the same today.

Champagne Kir Royale

Many people prefer this drink with only a small amount of Crème de Cassis (dry), so always ask before you make one!

1 teaspoon Crème de Cassis
4 ounces chilled Champagne

Pour the Crème de Cassis into a Champagne flute. Fill with Champagne.

Bellini Cocktail

2 ounces peach purée
6 ounces Champagne
$1/4$ ounce peach liqueur

Mix the purée and Champagne gently in a glass. Pour into a flute and top with the liqueur.

Champagne Mimosa

2 ounces orange juice
4 ounces Champagne

Pour the orange juice into a Champagne flute. Fill with Champagne.

French 75

This drink can also be served over ice in a white wine glass.

1½ ounces Brandy
½ ounce lemon juice
1 ounce Simple Syrup (page 63)
2 ounces chilled Champagne

Shake the Brandy, lemon juice and syrup with ice. Strain into a large cocktail glass. Fill with Champagne.

According to actor David Niven,
Champagne offers "a minimum of alcohol
and a maximum of companionship."

The *Affordable Luxury*

Weddings...Gifts
& Celebrations...
Opening...Storing

LeRoy Neiman

Storing Champagne

Proper storage is essential to maintaining the quality of the wine. Champagne should always be stored lying on its side, so that the wine stays in touch with the cork. The most important rule, though, is to keep Champagne at a constant temperature (42 degrees is ideal). Yes, you may keep it in the refrigerator, but preferably for no longer than two weeks. Of course, we know it is impossible for anyone to keep Champagne for two weeks!

Multivintage Champagnes are aged in the cellars of Champagne and are ready to drink upon arrival at the market. However, vintage Champagnes can be aged anywhere from five to ten years. One friend says: "My philosophy is...don't keep it! Drink it...unless you are fortunate enough to be a collector."

Opening Champagne

Most Champagne houses have a tab on the neck foil that allows you to pull and remove the foil in one motion. Otherwise, cut off the foil from the bottom.

With a towel in hand, unfasten and remove the wire muzzle. (I loosen the wire muzzle and leave on the foil to ensure a firmer grip.)

Once the wire muzzle is either removed or loosened, place a towel over the top of the bottle and keep your hand on top with a firm grip. Never take your hand off the top of the bottle or point the bottle in anyone's direction. The pressure of the cork in the bottle is three times the pressure in your car's tires—the cork could damage any object it hits.

Turn the bottle in one direction and the cork in the opposite direction and ease out the cork, with a light pop. This is music to everyone's ears, and you never hear only one.

Champagne Service in a Restaurant

The server should show the unopened bottle to the customer, to verify that it is the bottle that was ordered. After opening the bottle, the server should place the cork in front of the host or hostess. The server will then pour a small amount of Champagne into the flute for the customer to taste. This is to ensure that the wine is good and not corked or flat and to ensure that the wine is the right temperature.

A Most Unusual Service

Fish biologist Arthur DeVries, while stationed at McMurdo Sound in Antarctica, had a small birthday celebration. His wife (and colleague) served a fish from local waters as an hors d'oeuvre. Sipping Champagne with deep-fried mawsoni caught at 1,600 feet beneath the ice-covered sound, while looking out a picture window across fifty miles of Antarctic landscape, "was an unusual experience," said Mr. DeVries.

Champagne as a Gift

Champagne wines have earned a reputation for gaiety, grandeur, and universality, yet they are surprisingly affordable, making Champagne an ideal gift. Though practical for the gift-bearer, since Champagnes are priced between $25 and $150, a bottle of Champagne is a prestigious present for the receiver. Its sheer presence creates an event!

Jean-Louis Carbonnier, head of the Champagne Wines Information Bureau, says: "First and foremost great wines, Champagne wines come from La Champagne, France, where they have been produced for over three centuries. The wines were so sought after that they became one of the most exclusive presents to be made to loved ones, friends, and acquaintances."

Today, Champagne wines are enjoyed in approximately one hundred fifty countries worldwide. "And," adds Monsieur

Carbonnier, "the old French tradition of gift-giving with Champagne has spread with the excellence of the wines."

Here are a few possible suggestions to:

Remember loved ones: Six bottles of Classic Brut Champagne.

Put a twinkle in the eye of spouses and lovers: A bottle of Prestige Cuvée Rosé.

Honor hosts and hostesses at dinners and gatherings: A chilled bottle of Champagne for two, or maybe a magnum. You will be invited again!

Surprise collector friends and relatives: A Methuselah (eight bottles), Salmanazar (twelve bottles), or a Nebuchadnezzar (twenty bottles). What a show stopper!

Please in-laws: Vintage Champagnes. No doubt, the wines will be shared at a family dinner.

Acknowledge cousins for the summer cottage they so graciously lent: A case of Champagne.

Indulge friends: An assortment of Champagne wines and favorite goodies.

Thank business associates and everybody else:
Ready-packaged combinations, such as a
Champagne bottle and flutes; a bottle and an ice bucket; a set of
flutes or tulip glasses; a half-bottle basket;
Champagne books; or a selection of Champagne
wines. All these items are available from most
wine shops.

Additional ideas:

Give a twelve-bottle case of half-bottles and personalize them with
twelve different holidays, such as a birthday, Valentine's Day, May
Day, Fourth of July, and so forth.

Expand the idea and give a twenty-four bottle case of splits.
Compose your own clever sayings and anecdotes, such as, "when
you get through the day, you deserve a glass of Champagne!"

Champagne wines make gift-giving simple—affordable yet elegant.
Their unique qualities and universal appeal enliven any festivity.

Break Out the Bubbly

At the Harrison Conference Center in Glen Cove, New York, director of special events Barry Weisberg uses Champagne in several ways.

Guests are often offered a flute of Champagne as they enter the Harrison House mansion. "We greet guests with Champagne because the image of Champagne says 'celebration' and 'good times'; it sets the mood." Since everyone loves the sound of popping corks, he uses the effect to signal wedding guests that the toasts and cake-cutting are imminent. For a daytime wedding, guests are greeted with a salmanazar-sized bottle to sign instead of a guest register. Guests can even go home with a personalized split of bubbly as a wedding favor from the happy couple.

For those couples who prefer a less formal—but still elegant—reception, he offers a Champagne wedding brunch. And, after all the festivities have ended, the newlyweds can anticipate a Champagne breakfast in the bridal suite the following morning.

Oftentimes, the couple will return to Harrison House with their "crated salmanazar" and their bridal party for their first anniversary celebration.

Since Champagne can be dry or sweet, they have developed several food and pastry delights using Champagnes.

Lucky guests who attended a recent Champagne tasting event began to realize the everyday enjoyment that Champagne affords. Two typical Champagne tasting pairings are poached Norwegian salmon in a cornhusk with Southwestern relish, served with vintage Champagne; and tenderloin of veal stuffed with Montrachet and spinach, served with Rosé and non-vintage Champagne, followed by a wild-strawberry tart!

Pairings

Extravagant Uses of Champagne

There are many stories about famous Hollywood parties of the thirties with sparkling swimming pools filled with fabulous Champagne. Obviously, non-vintage is best suited for this extravagance, unless money truly is no object!

Marilyn Monroe was reported to have taken Champagne baths from time to time. (Rosé, of course, with a pink bathroom bathed in pink candle-light and pink bubbles!) Bubbles make both the skin and the spirit sparkle!!!!

One of my favorite Champagne extravagances comes from a Texas friend who had a private bowling alley in his home. For his annual Christmas party, he replaced the pins with Champagne bottles. The first person to make a Champagne strike was given a case of Champagne every month for the next year. (It could be a bottle every month, depending on your budget.)

113

What to Do with Those Empties

Don't throw them away—the bigger they are, the more collectible they are! Here are just a few suggestions.

CANDLES: Regular or unusual bottles make fabulous candles (once you've finished drinking the wonderful Champagne, of course!). You can purchase porcelain stoppers with oil wicks that fit Champagne bottles perfectly.

LAMPS: Interesting bottles with artwork and special vintages or packaging make great lamps and it's easy to have them wired.

DOORSTOPS: Bottles of three-liter size and larger make wonderful doorstops and conversation pieces.

BANKS: I have some salmanazar-sized banks—one for pennies and one for quarters.

VASES: Splits and half-bottles make wonderful vases for multiple or single flower arrangements.

PLACE CARDS: Splits (187's) make marvelous place cards for your dinner party. You can personalize them with the guest's name by writing on the glass in gold or silver. (Pens are available in any office supply store or art store.) These sizes are also wonderful wedding favors for guests—personalized, of course.

WEDDING CAKE: Another idea is to use splits as the tiers of your wedding cake, using identical Champagne in the batter.

BOOKENDS: Again, unusual bottles or vintages make any library more interesting.

Empties

*Legend has it that part of the reason Napoleon lost at Waterloo
was that his supply line to the Champagne cellars of Epernay
had been cut off, and he had instead been left to drink Belgian beer.*

Quips & Quotes

Quotes...
Toasts...
Glossary...
Reading List

Toasts have long been used to enhance the pleasure of drinking. In France, at the end of the sixteenth century, it was customary to place a piece of toast in the bottom of a wine glass. The glass was then passed from hand to hand until it reached the honored person whose health was being drunk. This gave rise to the expression "to drink a toast." Superstitious people clinked glasses because they were afraid the devil would enter their bodies with the wine, so they made a noise to scare him away. Today, lovers in France often intertwine forearms while sipping Champagne after a toast.

In 1959 Prince and Princess Guy de Polignac, of Champagne Pommery, gave a special luncheon at their chateau to honor Prince Rainier and Princess Grace. At each guest's place was a crystal pipe, with a tap, from which vintage Champagne could be drawn at will. Other Americans so honored have included Walt Disney and John F. Kennedy.

During Prohibition, Champagne could not legally be imported into the U.S. Yet, an estimated seventy-one million bottles entered the country—nearly a ten-year supply at the present rate of consumption (seven to eight million bottles annually). In 1959, a young couple found nine bottles washed up on a Cape Cod beach. The cork was dated 1920, and the Champagne was still sparkling.

———————————

Jelly Roll Morton was the pianist at Hilma Burt's place, a palace of pleasure in Storyville, New Orleans, where, he said, "Wine flowed much more than water—the kind of wine I am speaking about . . . I mean Champagne." At closing time, "It was my habit to pour partly finished wine together, then make up a new bottle from the mixture. That fine drink gave me a name (Wining Boy) and I wrote a tune from that which was very popular." In this sense, it might be said that Champagne helped celebrate the birth of jazz in the United States.

The word "Champagne" is of Latin derivation, going back to the time when Julius Caesar's Roman legions arrived unexpectedly in the rolling wooded hills ninety miles northeast of what is now Paris. Caesar and his men drilled and battled in an open field they called a "campus." Corrupted by the less-than-elegant soldiers, the word campus became "Campainia" in Latin; in French, "Champaign"—later to become "Champagne." This name was given to an ancient French province; it is also used for the sparkling wine produced in the region's 64,000 acres of vineyards.

In restaurants of the Champagne region, and in the dining rooms of the great Champagne Houses, wine stewards customarily pour Champagne with the thumb in the punt of the bottle and the fingers supporting the bottle along its length. As one of them explains, "One holds a bottle of red wine by the neck, a woman by the waist, and a bottle of Champagne by the derrière."

The saucer-shaped "coupe" glass, considered by many to be a poor vessel, badly suited to serving or drinking Champagne, originated as a porcelain mold of Marie Antoinette's breast. The queen adored Champagne, and the glass was a gallant salute to her good taste. In favoring the tulip- or flute-shaped glass because it retains the sparkle and aroma of the wine, Champagne connoisseurs suggest the saucer glass be used either for sherbet or by "those who like their Champagne and their woman flat."

King Edward VII of Britain, a great admirer of the ballerinas of Covent Garden, is credited with the legend of sipping Champagne from dancers' slippers. When the romantic king asked for a dancer's slipper and drank Champagne from it, he was intimating that he wanted to meet the young dancer later.

George Washington served Champagne to a senator from South Carolina in 1790. On March 4 of that year, a Senator Johnson wrote to Stephen Decatur: "I have just left the President's where I had the pleasure of dining with almost every member of the Senate. We had some excellent Champagne and after it I had the honour of drinking coffee with his lady, a most amiable woman."

_____

Although Champagne is identified with celebration, elegance, and friendship, the Champagne province has been the site of bitter conflict since Roman times. Over the centuries its fields have been trampled upon by invading Gallic tribesmen, Attila and his Huns, Clovis, the warrior chief of the Franks, and armies of Russians, Prussians, English, and Americans. When Napoleon was defeated, the Russians invaded France and the Champagne province was occupied by troops of the Czar. The Cossacks lived up to their reputation as heroic tipplers and drank deeply of the sparkling wine. From then until the Bolshevik Revolution, Imperialist Russia was Champagne's largest foreign consumer.

The "three musketeers" of Champagne were a trio of noblemen from the Champagne region: the Marquis de Saint-Evremond, the Comte d'Olonne, and the Marquis de Sillery. These gourmets "of refined and somewhat extravagant tastes" insisted on having the very best. They refused to drink any wines other than those of Ay, Avenay, Hautvillers. It was they who introduced Champagne into the court of Louis XIV; gossips in the king's retinue dubbed them *Les Côteaux* (the slopes). Saint-Evremond later was sent to England to congratulate Charles II upon his restoration to the throne; he eventually introduced Champagne to the Royal House in that country. To this day there exists in Champagne a gastronomic society called *l'Ordre des Côteaux de Champagne*, which traces its beginnings to these three noblemen.

The Champagne Glossary

Appellation: *Appellation d'origine contrôlée* or AOC—Legal designation guaranteeing a wine by geographical origin, grape variety, and production method.

Assemblage: Blending of still wines from different villages and often from different years, to create a "cuvée" or blend ready for bottling and second fermentation.

Autolysis: Enzymatic breakdown of dead yeast cells. This takes place in the wine after the second fermentation; it gives complexity of flavors.

Blanc de Blancs: Champagne made only from white Chardonnay grapes.

Blanc de Noirs: Champagne made only from black Pinot Noir and/or Meunier grapes.

Brut: Dry Champagne, containing not more than 15 grams per liter of residual sugar.

CIVC: *Comité Interprofessionnel du Vin de Champagne*—coordinating body which regulates grape growing and wine production in Champagne. It is headed by the president of Champagne Houses and the president of Champagne growers.

Cooperative: A union of Champagne growers.

Crémant: Style of Champagne with a less vigorous sparkle than normal. Since September 1994, this term is no longer used in Champagne, but is being used to designate AOC sparkling wines from other parts of France.

Cru: Literally, "growth"—used to signify the vineyards of a village. See also "premier cru" and "grand cru."

Cuvée: First 2,050 liters of juice pressed from each 4,000 kilos of grapes—the highest-quality juice. Also a finished blend, usually a combination of many crus and several vintages.

Cuvée de prestige: Top-of-the-line wine, usually vintage-dated, always more expensive.

Dégorgement: Removal from the bottle of yeast sediments left after the second fermentation; usually done "à la glace," by freezing the neck of the upended bottle so that the sediments form an icy plug that can then be easily ejected.

Demi-sec: Sweeter Champagne, containing between 33 and 50 grams of residual sugar per liter.

Dosage: Amount of sugar added to finished Champagne in the liqueur d'expédition; it governs final sweetness.

Dry/sec: Medium-sweet Champagne, containing between 17 and 35 grams of residual sugar per liter.

Échelle des crus: Quality classification system of the 312 villages in the Champagne region. See also "cru," "grand cru," and "premier cru."

Extra dry/Extra sec: Medium-dry Champagne, containing between 12 and 20 grams of residual sugar per liter.

Grand cru: Village rated at 100% on the "échelle des crus"; Champagne made entirely from grapes grown in these villages may be labeled "grand cru."

Grande marque: Term describing the members of the historic *syndicat de grandes marques,* established in 1882.

Lattes: Wooden slats used to separate layers of bottles during and after the second fermentation. During "sur lattes," aging, the wines develop depth and complexity from contact with the second fermentation lees.

Lees: Sediments, such as dead yeasts, deposited by a wine after fermentation (first and second).

Liqueur d'expédition: Solution of sugar and wine added to Champagne after disgorgement. See also "dosage."

Liqueur de tirage: Solution of sugar, wine and yeast added to the finished blend when it is bottled in order to provoke a second fermentation.

Maceration: One of two techniques used to color Rosé Champagnes. It involves steeping a part of the Pinot Noir or Meunier juice with the skins to leach out the color. See also "assemblage."

Malolactic fermentation: Not a true fermentation, but a bacteriological conversion of malic acid into lactic acid (and carbon dioxide), lowering the total acidity of a wine.

Marc: The capacity of a Champagne press, equivalent to 4,000 kg of grapes. Also, the debris of pips, skins, and stalks left after pressing; and the spirit distilled from this debris ("pomace").

Millésimé: See "Vintage Champagne."

Mousse: Froth of bubbles that results from the second fermentation in the bottle.

Must: Newly pressed grape juice which is ready for fermentation to begin.

Non millésimé: See "Non-vintage."

Non-vintage (NV): Champagne blended from several years and sold without a vintage date. Known in French as *non millésimé* or *sans année*.

Premier cru: Village rated between 90 and 99 percent on the "échelle des crus"; Champagne made entirely from grapes grown in such villages may be labeled "premier cru."

Prise de mousse: Process whereby Champagne acquires its sparkle; it takes place slowly during the second fermentation, inside the bottle.

Pupître: Two hinged boards containing 60 angled holes each, used for holding the bottles during "remuage."

Racking: Transferring wine from one container to another, to separate it from its lees.

Remuage: Riddling. The twisting, jolting, and gradual inversion of bottles in pupîtres; the aim is to gather the second fermentation deposits in the neck, ready for disgorgement.

Remueur: Worker charged exclusively with remuage.

Sans année: See "non-vintage."

Sec: See "dry."

Second fermentation: Fermentation that is provoked by the sugar and yeast in the "liqueur de tirage" and takes place inside the bottle. It causes the wine to sparkle.

Taille: Second portion of juice (500 liters) pressed from each 4,000 kg of grapes. "Taille" follows the "cuvée." Juice extracted beyond the "taille" cannot be used for Champagnes and will be distilled.

Vintage Champagne: Champagne made from the wine of a single, good-quality year. Also known as "millésimé."

Champagne Reading List

Champagne: The Wine, the Land and the People
Patrick Forbes

Champagne
Henry Nultly

Champagne & Caviar
Nicholas Von Wiesenberger

The Magic of Champagne
Andrew Jefford

Champagne
Tom Stevenson

Champagne: The History and the Character of the World's Most Celebrated Wine
Serena Sutcliffe

A History of Champagne
Henry Vizetelly

Champagne: The Spirit of Celebration
Sara Slavin and Karl Petzke

The Story of Champagne
Nicholas Faith